Into the Forest

Other great books in the series

zendoodle coloring

Calming Swirls

Cozy Cats

Creative Sensations

Enchanting Gardens

Inspiring Zendalas

zendoodle coloring

Into the Forest

Woodland Creatures to Color and Display

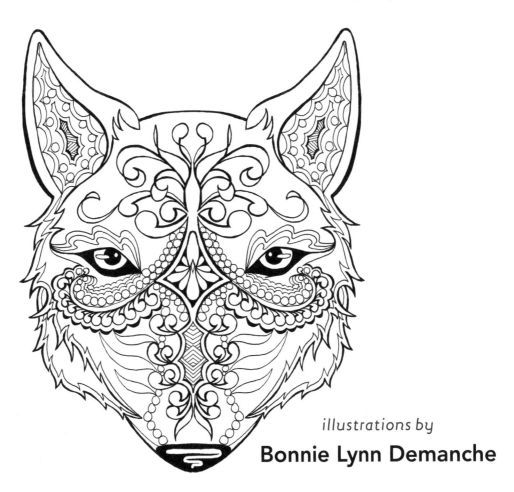

illustrations by

Bonnie Lynn Demanche

ST. MARTIN'S GRIFFIN

NEW YORK

ZENDOODLE COLORING: INTO THE FOREST.
Copyright © 2016 by St. Martin's Press. All rights reserved.
Printed in the United States of America. For information, address
St. Martin's Press, 175 Fifth Avenue, New York, N.Y. 10010.

www.stmartins.com

ISBN 978-1-250-10879-1 (trade paperback)

Our books may be purchased in bulk for promotional, educational, or business use.
Please contact your local bookseller or the Macmillan Corporate and Premium
Sales Department at 1-800-221-7945, extension 5442, or by e-mail
at MacmillanSpecialMarkets@macmillan.com.

First Edition: March 2016

10 9 8 7 6 5 4 3 2 1

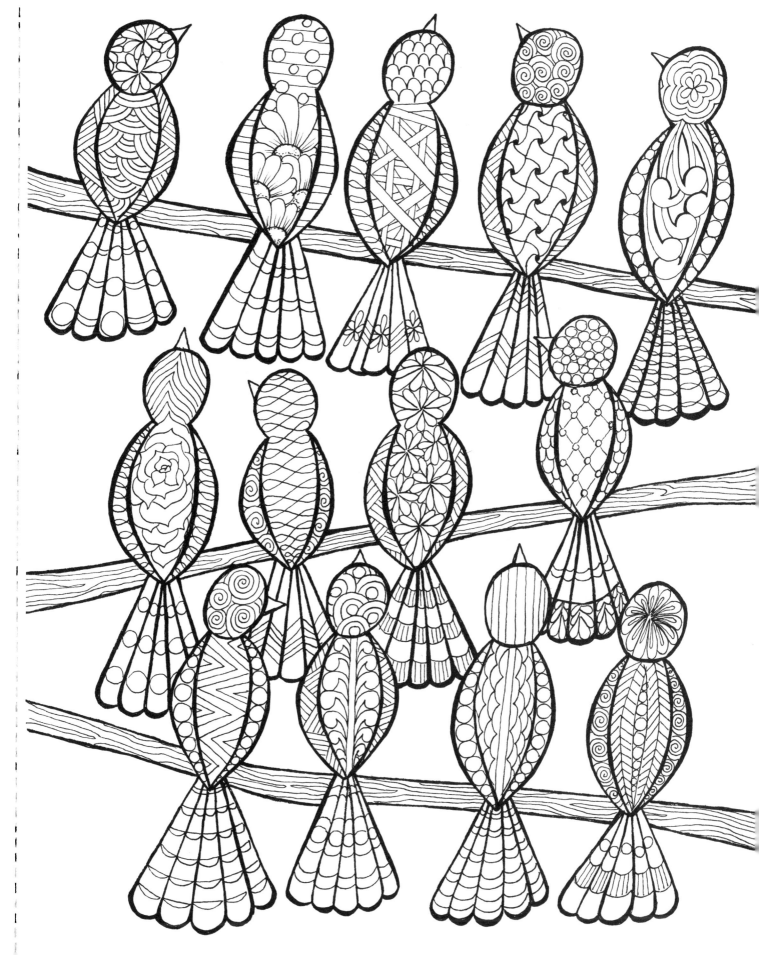

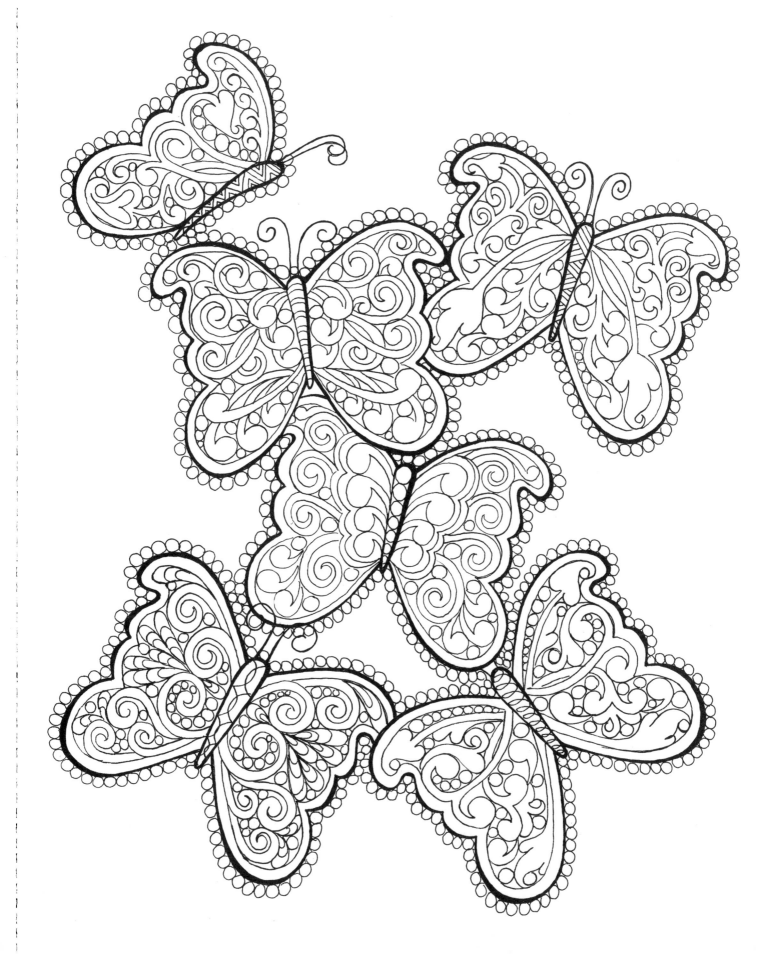

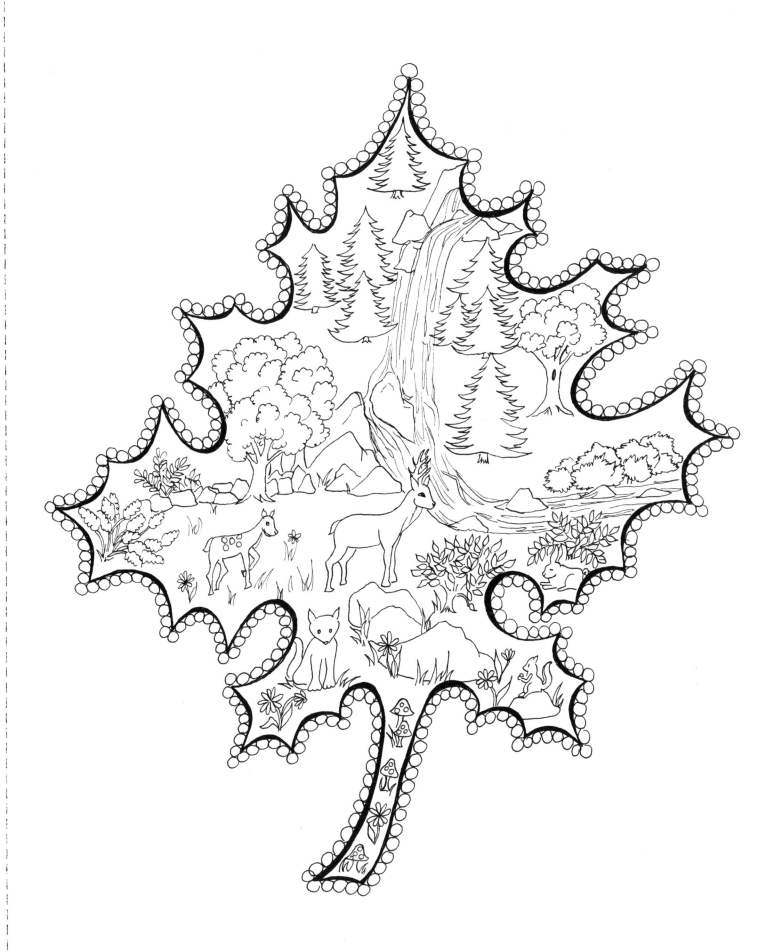

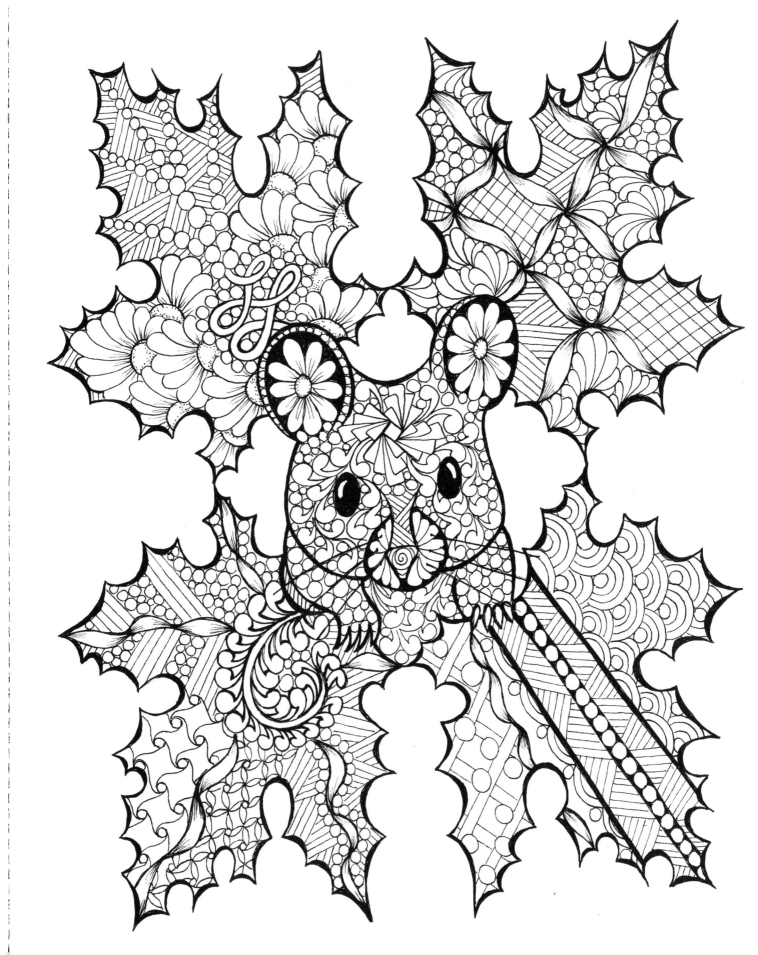

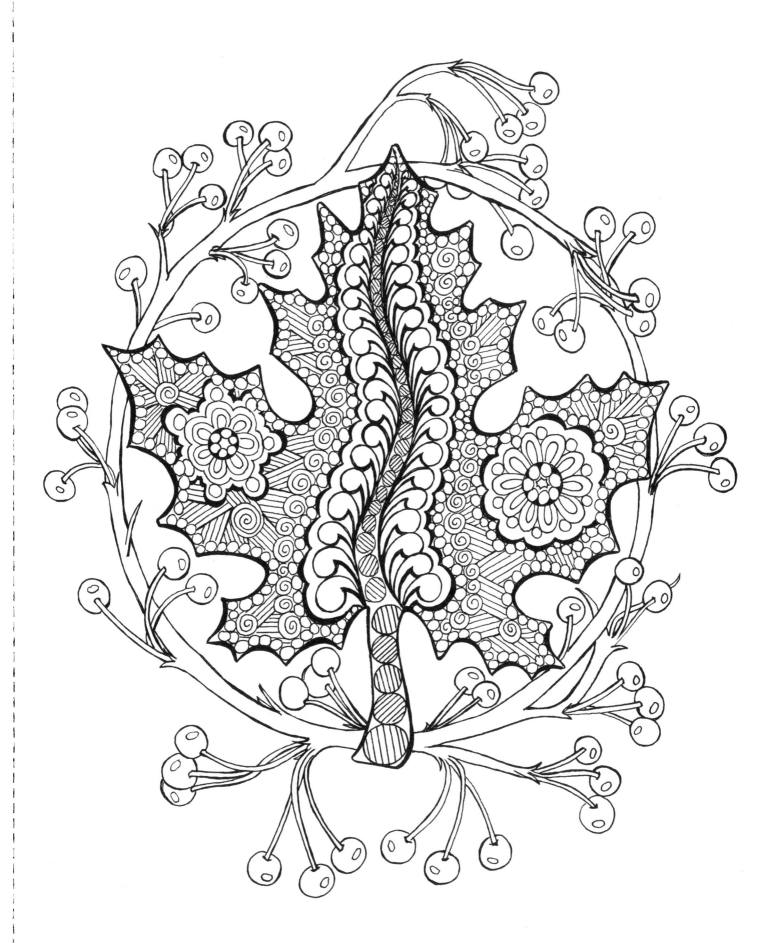

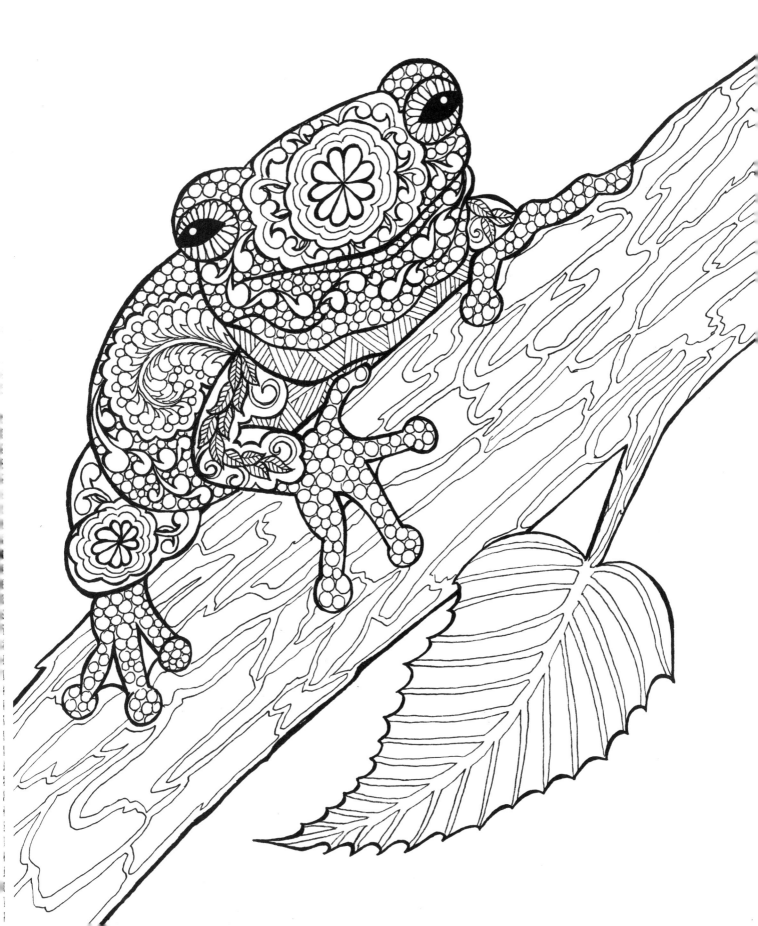

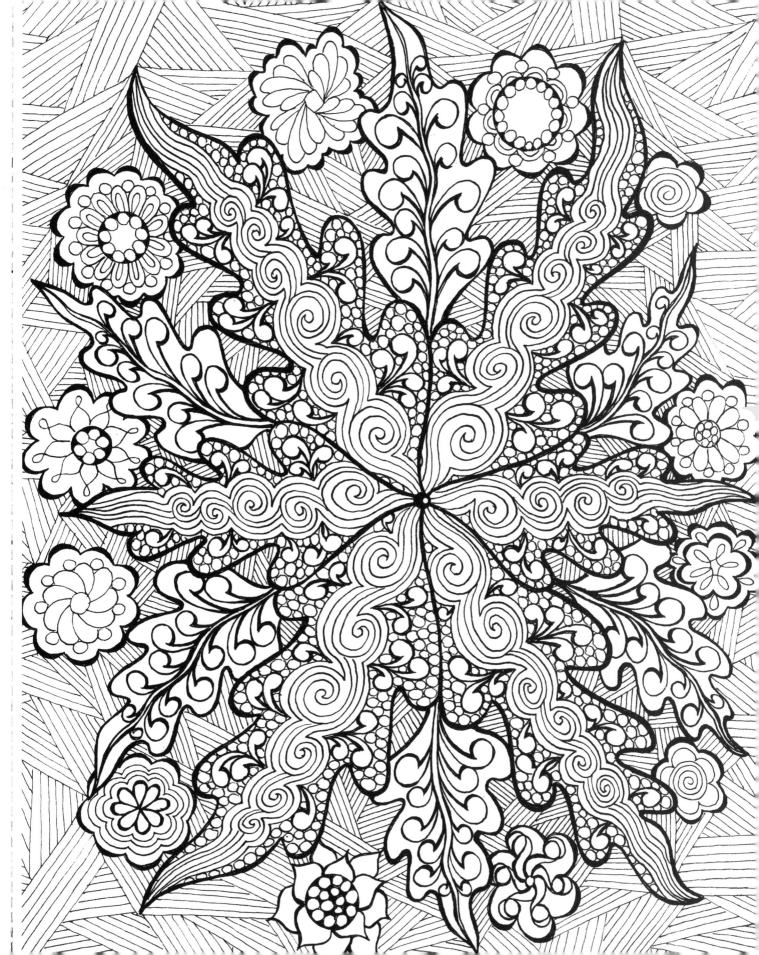